the burger book

Gina Steer

p

This is a Parragon Publishing Book
This edition published in 2005

Parragon Publishing
Queen Street House
4 Queen Street
Bath BA1 1HE
United Kingdom

Produced by
The Bridgewater Book Company
Lewes, East Sussex BN7 2NZ
United Kingdom

Photographer Emma Neish
Home Economist Joy Skipper

ISBN 1-40543-646-8
Printed in China

Notes for the reader
This book uses imperial, metric, or US cup measurements. Follow the same units of
measurement throughout; do not mix imperial and metric. All spoon measurements are level:
teaspoons are assumed to be 5 ml, and tablespoons are assumed to be 15 ml. Unless otherwise
stated, milk is assumed to be whole, eggs, and individual vegetables such as carrots are
medium, and pepper is freshly ground black pepper.

The times given for each recipe are an approximate guide only. The preparation times may
differ according to the techniques used by different people and the cooking times may vary
as a result of the type of oven used. Ovens should be preheated to the specified temperature.
If using a fan-assisted oven, check the manufacturer's instructions for adjusting the time
and temperature.

Recipes using raw eggs should be avoided by infants, the elderly, pregnant women,
convalescents, and anyone suffering from an illness.

introduction 4

fish 6

poultry 20

meat 36

vegetarian 62

drinks 84

index 96

contents

Burgers have to be one of the most universally popular convenience foods of all time, and around the world are served up as fast food. Now, however, they have made their way into fashionable restaurants as good quality food, using fresh ingredients and a range of imaginative toppings. The burgers in this book are made of fish, such as smoked trout, crab, and angler fish; poultry, including turkey and duck; meats such as pork, beef, and lamb; and a range of vegetarian options that use ingredients such as yams, squash, cornmeal, provolone, tofu, and macadamias.

These burgers use a tantalizing array of spices, herbs, flavorings, and relishes to enhance and embellish taste and texture. Using such a wide variety of ingredients it is possible to provide a different burger every day for more than a month. With the vast array of

introduction

ideas it is possible to serve a meal that will satisfy family and friends and, by varying the accompaniments and side dishes, a completely different taste and look can be achieved every time you serve them.

These burgers are simple to prepare and cook. However delicious, exotic, spicy, or fragrant the outcome, you just place the ingredients in a food processor and use the pulse button, or mix together in a bowl by hand, using either your fingers, a fork, or a wooden spoon.

The recipes come with serving and drink suggestions. For the health conscious, broil the burgers rather than pan-fry them and serve with baked or new potatoes or oven-baked french fries, griddled vegetables, fresh salads, homemade relishes, and salsas.

These recipes use a variety of fish, and each variety brings its own flavor and texture to the burger, ranging from smoky and spicy to Asian and fragrant. When combined with herbs, spices, and vegetables, the results are both healthy and mouthwateringly delicious. It is important to use really fresh fish that has a firm texture, such as salmon, angler fish or cod loin, rather than the more delicate sole or flounder. It is also better to use fillets that have been skinned and the pin bones removed. If using frozen fish, thaw thoroughly and pat dry with paper towels before use.

fish

Smoked fish and bacon may seem a strange combination, but they work really well together here, especially when teamed with the fresh and fragrant pesto relish.

smoky trout burgers with pesto relish

ingredients

8 oz/225 g potatoes, cut into chunks
salt and pepper
12 oz/350 g smoked trout fillets, flaked
2 tsp creamed horseradish
6 scallions, finely chopped
6 oz/175 g zucchini, coarsely grated
2 tbsp whole-wheat flour
8 lean Canadian bacon slices
2 tbsp corn oil

pesto relish
3 tbsp fresh basil
generous ¼ cup pine nuts, toasted
3 garlic cloves
⅔ cup virgin olive oil
1½ oz/40 g Parmesan cheese,
  freshly grated
1½-inch/4-cm piece cucumber, peeled
  and finely diced
4 scallions, finely chopped
2 plum tomatoes, finely diced

one Cook the potatoes in a pan of lightly salted water for 15–20 minutes, or until cooked. Drain, mash, and place in a large bowl. Add the trout, horseradish, scallions, zucchini, and salt and pepper to taste. Mix together and shape into 4 equal-size burgers. Let chill for 1 hour, then coat in the flour and wrap each in 2 slices of bacon.

two Meanwhile, prepare the relish. Place the basil, pine nuts, and garlic in a food processor and blend for 1 minute. With the motor running, gradually pour in the oil and continue to blend until all the oil has been incorporated. Scrape into a bowl and stir in the cheese, cucumber, scallions, and tomatoes. Spoon into a serving bowl.

three Heat a heavy-bottom skillet and add the oil. When hot, add the burgers and cook over medium heat for 3–4 minutes on each side until golden and piping hot. Serve.

recommended servings
Place on the bases of 4 ciabatta rolls with salad greens and charred red bell pepper wedges and a little Pesto Relish. Serve with iced tea or Fresh Lemonade (see page 89) and hand round the remaining relish separately.

Perked up with basil and fresh Parmesan, and served with a garlicky mayonnaise, these cod burgers are fantastically tasty. The cornmeal that holds all the ingredients together is very easy to prepare.

provençal cod burgers

ingredients

1¼ cups water

1½ cups instant cornmeal

1 lb/450 g cod fillet, skinned

1 tbsp chopped fresh basil

2 oz/55 g Parmesan cheese,
  freshly grated

salt and pepper

2 tbsp all-purpose flour

1–2 tbsp olive oil

aïoli

4 garlic cloves, crushed

2 egg yolks

2 tsp lemon juice

1¼ cups extra virgin olive oil

one Place the water in a large pan and bring to a boil. Slowly pour in the cornmeal in a steady stream and cook over gentle heat, stirring constantly, for 5 minutes, or until thick. Let cool for about 10 minutes.

two Place the cornmeal, fish, basil, cheese, and salt and pepper in a food processor and, using the pulse button, blend together. Shape into 4–6 burgers, then coat in the flour. Cover and let chill for 1 hour.

three Meanwhile, make the aïoli. Place the garlic and egg yolks in a food processor and blend for 1 minute. Add the lemon juice and blend again. With the motor running, slowly pour in the oil until a thick mayonnaise is formed. Add salt and pepper to taste and, if too thick, add a little extra lemon juice.

four Heat a heavy-bottom skillet and add 1 tablespoon of the oil. When hot, add the burgers and cook over medium heat for 4–5 minutes on each side or until cooked through, adding extra oil if necessary. Serve.

Note

Recipes using raw eggs should be avoided by infants, the elderly, pregnant women, convalescents, and anyone suffering from an illness.

recommended servings

Split 4–6 thick wedges of focaccia and arrange fresh spinach leaves and a burger on top. Spoon over a little Aïoli. Serve with the other half of focaccia, some roasted Mediterranean vegetables, and a glass of dry white wine or Fresh Lemonade (see page 89).

These are a really delicious treat and have a spicy Asian flavor. Canned crabmeat is fine, but if you are able to use fresh crabmeat the results will be even more special.

thai crab burgers with bean sprouts

ingredients

1½ tbsp corn oil

1 fresh red chili, seeded and finely chopped

1-inch/2.5-cm piece fresh gingerroot, grated

2 lemon grass stalks, outer leaves removed and finely chopped

12 oz/350 g canned white crabmeat, drained and flaked

8 oz/225 g cooked shelled shrimp, thawed if frozen and squeezed dry

2½ cups cooked Thai rice

1 tbsp chopped fresh cilantro

¾ cup bean sprouts

6 scallions, finely chopped

1 tbsp soy sauce

1–2 tbsp whole-wheat flour

one Heat a wok or skillet and when hot add 2 teaspoons of the oil, the chili, ginger, and lemon grass and stir-fry over medium-high heat for 1 minute. Remove the wok from the heat and let cool.

two Place the chili mixture, crabmeat, shrimp, rice, chopped cilantro, bean sprouts, scallions, and soy sauce in a food processor and, using the pulse button, blend together. Shape into 4 equal-size burgers, then coat in the flour. Cover and let chill for 1 hour.

three Heat a heavy-bottom, nonstick skillet and add the remaining oil. When hot, add the burgers and cook over medium heat for 3–4 minutes on each side or until piping hot. Serve.

recommended servings
Place some shredded napa cabbage and fresh bean sprouts on the bases of 4 toasted sesame seed buns, top with the burgers, and drizzle over some sweet chili sauce. Place the lid in position and serve with a glass of Fresh Lemonade (see page 89).

prepare 15 minutes, plus 1 hour chilling
cook 25–35 minutes *serves* 4–6

Fresh salmon, spinach, and pine nuts create a very colorful burger. Be sure to squeeze as much water as possible out of the fresh spinach, otherwise the burgers may be rather soggy.

crispy salmon burgers with pine nuts

ingredients

10½ oz/300 g potatoes,
   cut into chunks
salt and pepper
1 lb/450 g fresh salmon fillet, skinned
3¾ cups fresh spinach leaves
⅜ cup pine nuts, toasted
2 tbsp finely grated lemon rind

1 tbsp chopped fresh parsley
2 tbsp whole-wheat flour
scant 1 cup sour cream
1½-inch/4-cm piece cucumber, peeled
   and finely chopped
2 tbsp corn oil

one Cook the potatoes in a pan of lightly salted boiling water for 15–20 minutes, or until tender. Drain well, then mash and set aside. Chop the salmon into chunks.

two Reserve a few spinach leaves for serving, then blanch the remainder in a pan of boiling water for 2 minutes. Drain, squeezing out any excess moisture, then chop.

three Place the spinach in a food processor with the salmon, potatoes, pine nuts, 1 tablespoon of the lemon rind, parsley, and salt and pepper and, using the pulse button, blend together. Shape into 4–6 equal-size burgers, then cover and let chill for 1 hour. Coat the burgers in the flour.

four Mix the sour cream, remaining lemon rind, and cucumber together in a bowl, then cover and let chill until required.

five Heat a heavy-bottom skillet and add the oil. When hot, add the burgers and cook for 4–6 minutes on each side or until piping hot. Serve.

recommended servings
Place the reserved spinach leaves on 4–6 whole-wheat buns, top with the burgers, then spoon over a little of the sour cream mixture and place the lid in position. Serve with griddled vine cherry tomatoes and Fresh Lemonade (see page 89).

Fresh tuna, chili, and mango are united in a totally modern burger. Tuna is best eaten slightly pink as it can be rather dry if overcooked. It is also important that the burgers are piping hot before serving.

fresh tuna burgers with mango salsa

ingredients

8 oz/225 g sweet potatoes, chopped
salt
1 lb/450 g fresh tuna steaks
6 scallions, finely chopped
6 oz/175 g zucchini, grated
1 fresh red jalapeño chili, seeded and
  finely chopped
2 tbsp prepared mango chutney
1 tbsp corn oil

mango salsa
1 large ripe mango, peeled and seeded
2 ripe tomatoes, finely chopped
1 fresh red jalapeño chili, seeded and
  finely chopped
1½-inch/4-cm piece cucumber,
  finely diced
1 tbsp chopped fresh cilantro
1–2 tsp honey

one Cook the sweet potatoes in a pan of lightly salted boiling water for 15–20 minutes, or until tender. Drain well, then mash and place in a food processor. Cut the tuna into chunks and add to the potatoes.

two Add the scallions, zucchini, chili, and mango chutney to the food processor and, using the pulse button, blend together. Shape into 4–6 equal-size burgers, then cover and let chill for 1 hour.

three Meanwhile make the salsa. Slice the mango flesh, reserving 8 good slices for serving. Finely chop the remainder, then mix with the tomatoes, chili, cucumber, cilantro, and honey. Mix well, then spoon into a small bowl. Cover and let stand for 30 minutes to allow the flavors to develop.

four Heat a heavy-bottom skillet and add the oil. When hot, add the burgers and cook over medium heat for 4–6 minutes on each side or until piping hot. Serve.

recommended servings
Place some salad greens on 4–6 halved wedges of cornbread, top with slices of reserved mango, then the burger. Spoon over a little salsa and serve with the other half of bread and a glass of Tropical Crush (see page 93).

prepare 15 minutes, plus 1 hour chilling
cook 25–30 minutes *serves* 4

These burgers have a wonderful subtle smoky flavor due to the addition of smoked haddock. If you prefer, other smoked fish, such as cod or mackerel, would also work well.

fish burgers

ingredients

5 oz/140 g potatoes, cut into chunks
salt and pepper
8 oz/225 g cod fillet, skinned
8 oz/225 g smoked haddock, skinned
1 tbsp grated lemon rind

1 tbsp chopped fresh parsley
1–2 tbsp all-purpose flour
1 egg, beaten
1½ cups fresh white bread crumbs
2 tbsp corn oil

one Cook the potatoes in a pan of lightly salted boiling water for 15–20 minutes, or until tender. Drain well and mash. Chop the fish into small pieces, then place in a food processor with the mashed potatoes, lemon rind, parsley, and salt and pepper to taste. Using the pulse button, blend together. Shape into 4 equal-size burgers and coat in the flour. Cover and let chill for 30 minutes.

two Place the egg and bread crumbs in 2 separate bowls and coat the burgers first in the egg, allowing any excess to drip back into the bowl, then in the bread crumbs. Let chill for an additional 30 minutes.

three Heat a heavy-bottom skillet and add the oil. When hot, add the burgers and cook over medium heat for 4–5 minutes on each side or until golden and cooked through. Serve.

recommended servings
Place a few lettuce leaves on the bases of 4 lightly toasted whole-wheat buns, top with a burger, and a squeeze of tomato ketchup. Add the lid and serve with coleslaw, extra tomato ketchup, french fries, and a Chocolate Milk Shake (see page 87).

The recipes in this chapter feature burgers made from chicken, turkey, and duck, and use an array of delicious herbs, spices, and fruits for extra flavor.

It is essential to cook chicken and turkey thoroughly. When cooked over too high a heat, there is a risk that the outside of the burger could start charring before the inside is heated through. If in doubt, make a small slit in the center of the burger and gently pull apart to check for pinkness in the middle. If the chicken or turkey is still a bit pink, continue cooking over gentler heat until it is completely cooked.

poultry

These deliciously tender, thin pieces of breaded chicken, served in a classic sesame seed bun with ketchup or mayonnaise, will go down very well with all the chicken and burger enthusiasts you know.

the ultimate chicken burger

ingredients

4 large chicken breast fillets, skinned

1 large egg white

1 tbsp cornstarch

1 tbsp all-purpose flour

1 egg, beaten

1 cup fresh white bread crumbs

2 tbsp corn oil

2 beefsteak tomatoes, sliced

one Place the chicken breasts between 2 sheets of nonstick parchment paper and flatten slightly using a meat mallet or a rolling pin. Beat the egg white and cornstarch together, then brush over the chicken. Cover and let chill for 30 minutes, then coat in the flour.

two Place the egg and bread crumbs in 2 separate bowls and coat the burgers first in the egg, allowing any excess to drip back into the bowl, then in the bread crumbs.

three Heat a heavy-bottom skillet and add the oil. When hot, add the burgers and cook over medium heat for 6–8 minutes on each side, or until thoroughly cooked. If you are in doubt, it is worth cutting one of the burgers in half. If there is any sign of pinkness, cook for a little longer. Add the tomato slices for the last 1–2 minutes of the cooking time to heat through. Serve.

recommended servings

Place some shredded romaine lettuce on the base of 4 toasted sesame seed buns. Top with the burger, then the sliced tomatoes. Spoon over a little tomato ketchup or mayonnaise and place the lid in position. Serve with french fries and Mango Smoothie (see page 91).

prepare 10 minutes, plus 1 hour chilling
cook 10–12 minutes *serves* 4

There are many varieties of fresh chilies available. If you are in doubt as to the chili's heat, then start with the milder chilies, such as jalapeño, and gradually move onto the hotter ones.

mexican turkey burgers

ingredients

1 lb/450 g fresh ground turkey

7 oz/200 g canned refried beans

2–4 garlic cloves, crushed

1–2 fresh jalapeño chilies, seeded and finely chopped

2 tbsp tomato paste

1 tbsp chopped fresh cilantro

salt and pepper

1 tbsp corn oil

one Place the ground turkey in a bowl and break up any large lumps. Beat the refried beans until smooth, then add to the turkey in the bowl.

two Add the garlic, chilies, tomato paste, cilantro, salt, and pepper and mix together. Shape into 4 equal-size burgers, then cover and let chill for 1 hour.

three Heat a heavy-bottom skillet and add the oil. When hot, add the burgers and cook over medium heat for 5–6 minutes on each side, or until thoroughly cooked. Drain on paper towels and serve.

recommended servings
Place some shredded spinach on the base of 4 toasted cheese-topped buns, top with the burgers, then spoon over some salsa and guacamole. Place the lid in position and serve with tortilla chips and iced tea or Ginger Beer (see page 95).

prepare 10 minutes, plus 1 hour chilling
cook 10–12 minutes *serves* 4

You can alter the flavor and texture of these luscious burgers by replacing the pine nuts with slivered almonds or unsalted cashews. If using whole nuts, chop them first and, if liked, toast lightly.

bacon-wrapped chicken burgers

ingredients

1 lb/450 g fresh ground chicken
1 onion, grated
2 garlic cloves, crushed
⅜ cup pine nuts, toasted
2 oz/55 g Gruyère cheese, grated

2 tbsp fresh snipped chives
salt and pepper
2 tbsp whole-wheat flour
8 lean Canadian bacon slices
1–2 tbsp corn oil

one Place the ground chicken, onion, garlic, pine nuts, cheese, chives, and salt and pepper to taste in a food processor. Using the pulse button, blend the mixture together using short sharp bursts. Scrape out onto a board and shape into 4 equal-size burgers. Coat in the flour, then cover and let chill for 1 hour.

two Wrap each burger with 2 bacon slices, securing in place with a wooden toothpick.

three Heat a heavy-bottom skillet and add the oil. When hot, add the burgers and cook over medium heat for 5–6 minutes on each side or until thoroughly cooked through. Serve.

recommended servings
Arrange some shredded iceberg lettuce and thinly sliced red onion on the bases of 4 ciabatta rolls. Top with a burger and a spoonful of mayonnaise. Finish with a few snipped fresh chives. Place on the lids and serve with coleslaw and a glass of Fresh Lemonade (see page 89).

What a healthy combination of ingredients there is in these burgers. Turkey and tarragon contribute fine, distinctive flavors, while the robust bulgur wheat is there for its nutty taste and coarse texture.

turkey and tarragon burgers

ingredients

generous ⅓ cup bulgur wheat
salt and pepper
1 lb/450 g fresh ground turkey
1 tbsp finely grated orange rind
1 red onion, finely chopped

1 yellow bell pepper, seeded, peeled, and finely chopped
¼ cup toasted slivered almonds
1 tbsp chopped fresh tarragon
1–2 tbsp corn oil

one Cook the bulgur wheat in a pan of lightly salted boiling water for 10–15 minutes, or according to the package instructions.

two Drain the bulgur wheat and place in a bowl with the ground turkey, orange rind, onions, yellow bell pepper, almonds, tarragon, and salt and pepper. Mix together, then shape into 4 equal-size burgers. Cover and let chill for 1 hour.

three Heat a heavy-bottom skillet and add the oil. When hot, add the burgers and cook over medium heat for 5–6 minutes on each side or until thoroughly cooked through. Drain well on paper towels and serve.

recommended servings
Place a few lettuce leaves on 4 plates. Cut 2 large baked potatoes in half and place one half on each plate. Top with the burgers. Spoon over a little red tomato relish or onion marmalade and serve with a tomato and onion salad and a glass of Ginger Beer (see page 95).

These delicious burgers are the perfect choice for an informal supper or lunch party. If you do not have a grinder, place the skinned duck breasts in a food processor and use the pulse button to chop.

duck burgers with sweet apple and plum relish

ingredients

2 Granny Smith or other eating apples

1 lb/450 g fresh duck breast meat, fat removed and ground

1 tbsp prepared Thai plum sauce

6 scallions, finely chopped

2 garlic cloves, crushed

1–1½ tsp dried crushed chilies

scant ⅜ cup dried cranberries

salt and pepper

1 tbsp butter

2–3 tsp raw brown sugar

sweet apple and plum relish

⅔ cup prepared apple sauce

2 tbsp prepared Thai plum sauce

one Peel, core, and grate 1 of the apples and place in a large bowl with the ground duck, plum sauce, scallions, garlic, ½–1 teaspoon of chilies, half the cranberries, and salt and pepper to taste. Mix together, then shape into 4 equal-size burgers. Cover and let chill for 1 hour.

two Preheat the broiler to medium-high. Place the burgers on a foil-lined broiler rack and cook under the hot broiler for 4–5 minutes on each side or until cooked to personal preference. Keep warm.

three Peel, core, and slice the remaining apple. Melt the butter in a skillet. Add the apple, sprinkle with the sugar, and cook for 3–4 minutes, or until slightly softened and lightly caramelized. Remove the skillet from the heat.

four To make the relish, heat the apple sauce, remaining chilies, cranberries, and the plum sauce for 3 minutes, stirring occasionally. Keep warm until ready to serve with the burgers.

recommended servings

Place some scallion and chili-flavored potato mash in the center of 4 warmed serving plates, top with the burgers, then the apple slices, and spoon over a little of the relish. Serve with a glass of Tropical Crush (see page 93).

prepare 15 minutes, plus 1 hour chilling
cook 20 minutes *serves* 4

To give the meal an authentic taste of the American deep south, serve these burgers with corn fritters and sautéed banana. When cooking bananas toss in lemon juice to help preserve their color.

maple-glazed turkey burgers

ingredients

2 ears fresh corn with leaves intact
1 lb/450 g fresh ground turkey
1 red bell pepper, seeded, peeled, and finely chopped
6 scallions, finely chopped
1 cup fresh white bread crumbs

2 tbsp chopped fresh basil
salt and pepper
1 tbsp corn oil
2 tbsp maple syrup

one Heat a grill pan until hot, then add the ears fresh corn and cook over medium-high heat for 8–10 minutes, turning every 2–3 minutes, or until the leaves are charred. Remove from the grill pan, let cool, then strip off the leaves and silky threads. Using a sharp knife, cut away the kernels and place in a bowl.

two Add the ground turkey, red bell pepper, scallions, bread crumbs, basil, salt, and pepper to the corn kernels in the bowl. Mix together, then shape into 4 equal-size burgers. Cover and let chill for 1 hour.

three Heat a heavy-bottom skillet and add the oil. When hot, add the burgers, then pour 1 teaspoon of maple syrup over each burger and cook over medium heat for 4 minutes. Turn the burgers over and cook for an additional 4–5 minutes, or until the burgers are cooked through. Pour over the remaining maple syrup and serve.

recommended servings
Lightly toast 4 cheese-topped buns and cover the bases with sprigs of arugula and watercress. Top with sliced tomato, the burgers, and corn relish. Accompany with corn fritters, sautéed banana, and a glass of Ginger Beer (see page 95).

prepare 12 minutes, plus 1 hour chilling
cook 20–30 minutes *serves* 4

Mixing some bacon into the ground chicken suffuses the burgers with extra flavor and ensures that they stay wonderfully succulent. Just go easy on the salt when you are seasoning the mixture.

chicken and bacon burgers

ingredients

12 oz/350 g Canadian bacon slices, rind removed
1½ cups fresh ground chicken
6 shallots
2–4 garlic cloves

1 tbsp tomato paste
1 tbsp chopped fresh parsley
salt and pepper
2 tbsp whole-wheat flour
1 tbsp corn oil

one Preheat the broiler to high. Cook 8 oz/225 g of the bacon under the hot broiler for 5–8 minutes, or until crisp. Remove and let cool.

two Place the broiled bacon in a food processor and add the ground chicken, shallots, and garlic. Using the pulse button, chop finely. Add the tomato paste, parsley, and salt and pepper and process for 1–2 minutes, or until blended. Scrape onto a board and shape into 4 equal-size burgers. Coat in the flour, then cover and let chill for 1 hour.

three Heat a heavy-bottom skillet and add the oil. When hot, add the burgers and cook over medium heat for 5–6 minutes on each side or until thoroughly cooked through. Meanwhile, preheat the broiler again and cook the remaining bacon for 5–8 minutes, or until crisp. Serve.

recommended servings

Arrange some salad greens on the bases of 4 toasted whole-wheat bun bases. Top with the burgers and the bacon, and spoon over a little cranberry sauce. Add the lid and serve with freshly cooked french fries and a Chocolate Milk Shake (see page 87).

When we think of burgers we tend to think of the standard hamburger or cheeseburger, served up on a bun with relish. Though these are delicious in their own right, the burgers in this chapter are oozing taste and imagination, showing influences as wide-ranging as Cajun, Mexican, and Greek. All the meats in these recipes are interchangeable. Always buy the best quality meat available and buy the lean cuts such as tenderloin, fillet, and top round. If you do not have a grinder, ask your butcher to grind the meat for you. Beef and lamb can be eaten slightly pink, but pork always needs to be thoroughly cooked through.

meat

The Cajun seasoning really livens up the flavor of these pork burgers. You should keep this seasoning in a cool, dark place. If exposed to heat or light, its pungency quickly disappears.

barbecued cajun pork burgers

ingredients

8 oz/225 g sweet potatoes,
  cut into chunks
salt and pepper
1 lb/450 g fresh ground pork
1 Granny Smith or other eating apple,
  peeled, cored, and grated

2 tsp Cajun seasoning
1 lb/450 g onions
1 tbsp chopped fresh cilantro
2 tbsp corn oil
8 lean Canadian bacon slices

one Cook the sweet potato in a pan of lightly salted boiling water for 15–20 minutes, or until soft when pierced with a fork. Drain well, then mash and set aside.

two Place the ground pork in a bowl, add the mashed potato, grated apple, and Cajun seasoning. Grate 1 of the onions and add to the pork mixture with salt and pepper to taste and the chopped cilantro. Mix together, then shape into 4–6 equal-size burgers. Cover and let chill for 1 hour.

three Preheat the barbecue. Slice the remaining onions. Heat 1 tablespoon of the oil in a skillet. Add the onions and cook over low heat for 10–12 minutes, stirring until soft. Remove the skillet from the heat and set aside. Wrap each burger in 2 slices of bacon.

four Cook the burgers over hot coals, brushing with the remaining oil for 4–5 minutes on each side, or until thoroughly cooked. Alternatively, cook the burgers in a skillet.

recommended servings
Serve each burger with sautéed onions on top of some Hoppin' John rice (rice cooked with scallions, thyme, hot pepper sauce, black-eye peas, and ham), with coleslaw and tomato ketchup and a glass of iced tea or Ginger Beer (see page 95).

The piquant flavor of orange juice and rind is the making of this burger. Even the large pieces of orange peel in the marmalade play their part by adding extra texture.

pork burgers with tangy orange marinade

ingredients

1 lb/450 g pork fillet, cut into
  small pieces
3 tbsp Seville orange marmalade
2 tbsp orange juice
1 tbsp balsamic vinegar
8 oz/225 g parsnips, cut into chunks

1 tbsp finely grated orange rind
2 garlic cloves, crushed
6 scallions, finely chopped
1 zucchini (6 oz/175 g), grated
salt and pepper
1 tbsp corn oil

one Place the pork in a shallow dish. Place the marmalade, orange juice, and vinegar in a small pan and heat, stirring, until the marmalade has melted. Pour the marinade over the pork. Cover and let stand for at least 30 minutes, or longer if time permits. Remove the pork, reserving the marinade. Grind the pork into a large bowl.

two Meanwhile, cook the parsnips in a pan of boiling water for 15–20 minutes, or until cooked. Drain, then mash and add to the pork. Stir in the orange rind, garlic, scallions, zucchini, and salt and pepper to taste. Mix together, then shape into 4–6 equal-size burgers. Cover and let chill for at least 30 minutes.

three Heat a heavy-bottom skillet and add the oil. When hot, add the burgers and cook over medium heat for 4–6 minutes on each side or until thoroughly cooked. Boil the reserved marinade for 3 minutes, then pour into a small pitcher or bowl. Serve.

recommended servings

Place some bitter salad greens on the bases of 4–6 toasted sesame seed buns, top with the burgers, pour over a little of the marinade, then add the lid. Serve with charred orange wedges, new potatoes, mixed salad, and a glass of Tropical Crush (see page 93).

prepare 10 minutes, plus 30 minutes' chilling
cook 8 minutes *serves* 4–6

These burgers are absolutely delicious—the combination of the feta cheese with the prunes, pine nuts, and rosemary may sound rather unusual, but tastes fabulous.

lamb and feta cheese burgers

ingredients

1 lb/450 g fresh ground lamb
8 oz/225 g feta cheese, crumbled
2 garlic cloves, crushed
6 scallions, finely chopped
½ cup no-soak prunes, chopped

2 tbsp pine nuts, toasted
1 cup fresh whole-wheat bread crumbs
1 tbsp chopped fresh rosemary
salt and pepper
1 tbsp corn oil

one Place the ground lamb in a large bowl with the cheese, garlic, scallions, prunes, pine nuts, and bread crumbs. Mix well, breaking up any lumps of meat.

two Add the rosemary and salt and pepper to the lamb mixture in the bowl. Mix together, then shape into 4–6 equal-size burgers. Cover and let chill for 30 minutes.

three Preheat the broiler to medium. Place the burgers on a foil-lined broiler rack and brush lightly with oil. Cook under the hot broiler for 4 minutes before turning over and brushing with the remaining oil. Continue to cook for 4 minutes, or until cooked to personal preference. Serve.

recommended servings

Arrange the spinach leaves on 4–6 serving plates and top with some freshly prepared couscous. Top with the burgers and spoon over a little tzatziki and serve with a Greek salad and a Melon Smoothie (see page 91).

prepare 10 minutes, plus 30 minutes' chilling
cook 16–20 minutes *serves* 4–6

Lamb and fresh mint are a classic partnership, which is greatly enhanced here by the introduction of sweet bell peppers, rich eggplant, and a little pungent Parmesan cheese.

minty lamb burgers

ingredients

1 red bell pepper, seeded and cut into quarters
1 yellow bell pepper, seeded and cut into quarters
1 red onion, cut into thick wedges
1 baby eggplant (4 oz/115 g), cut into wedges

2 tbsp olive oil
1 lb/450 g fresh ground lamb
2 tbsp freshly grated Parmesan cheese
1 tbsp chopped fresh mint
salt and pepper

one Preheat the broiler to medium. Place the bell peppers, onion, and eggplant on a foil-lined broiler rack, brush the eggplant with 1 tablespoon of the oil and cook under the hot broiler for 10–12 minutes, or until charred. Remove from the broiler, let cool, then peel the bell peppers. Place all the vegetables in a food processor and, using the pulse button, chop.

two Add the ground lamb, Parmesan cheese, chopped mint, and salt and pepper to the food processor and blend until the mixture comes together. Scrape onto a board and shape into 4–6 equal-size burgers. Cover and let chill for at least 30 minutes.

three Preheat the broiler to medium. Lightly brush the burgers with the remaining oil, then place on a foil-lined rack and cook under the hot broiler for 3–4 minutes on each side or until cooked to personal preference. Serve.

recommended servings
Blend 4 tablespoons of mayonnaise with 1 teaspoon of Dijon mustard and 1 tablespoon of chopped fresh mint. Serve the burgers on lettuce greens on the bases of 4–6 toasted sesame seed buns. Spoon on a little of the prepared mayonnaise and place the lid in position.

Bring out the best of the spicy flavors wrapped up in these curried burgers by serving them with the traditional Indian accompaniments—raita, lime pickle, and naan bread.

lamb tikka masala burgers

ingredients

scant ½ cup basmati rice
salt
5 cups fresh spinach leaves
1 lb/450 g fresh ground lamb
2 tbsp prepared tikka masala sauce

1 tbsp prepared mango chutney, plus
  extra for serving
2 tbsp toasted slivered almonds
1 tbsp corn oil

one Cook the rice in a pan of lightly salted boiling water for 10–12 minutes, or until cooked. Drain and place in a bowl.

two Reserve a few spinach leaves for serving and finely chop the remainder. Add to the rice together with the ground lamb and mix well.

three Add the tikka masala sauce, mango chutney, and almonds to the lamb mixture and mix together. Shape into 4–6 equal-size burgers, then cover and let chill for at least 30 minutes.

four Heat a heavy-bottom skillet and add the oil. When hot, add the burgers and cook over medium heat for 3–4 minutes on each side or until cooked to personal preference. Serve with the reserved spinach leaves.

recommended servings
Serve each burger on a bed of pilau rice with raita and lime pickle, naan bread, and a glass of Ginger Beer (see page 95).

prepare 10 minutes, plus 30 minutes' chilling
cook 16–25 minutes   *serves* 4–6

To experience the classic hamburger you have to make it with the finest quality ground meat and serve it in a traditional sesame seed bun with caramelized onions and some tomato ketchup.

the classic hamburger

ingredients

1 lb/450 g rump steak or top round, freshly ground

1 onion, grated

2–4 garlic cloves, crushed

2 tsp whole-grain mustard

pepper

2 tbsp olive oil

1 lb/450 g onions, finely sliced

2 tsp brown sugar

one Place the ground steak, onion, garlic, mustard, and pepper in a large bowl and mix together. Shape into 4–6 equal-size burgers, then cover and let chill for 30 minutes.

two Meanwhile, heat the oil in a heavy-bottom skillet. Add the onions and sauté over low heat for 10–15 minutes, or until the onions have caramelized. Add the sugar after 8 minutes and stir occasionally during cooking. Drain well on paper towels and keep warm.

three Wipe the skillet clean, then heat until hot. When hot, add the burgers and cook for 3–5 minutes on each side or until cooked to personal preference. Serve with the onions.

recommended servings

Arrange some shredded lettuce on the bases of 4–6 toasted sesame seed buns. Top with the burgers and then the onions. Spoon over a little tomato ketchup and serve with chunky style french fries and a Chocolate Milk Shake (see page 87).

A blend of soy sauce, wine, vinegar, various spices, and a hint of sweetness, teriyaki sauce is used as a marinade to tenderize the beef and infuse it with some Asian flavors.

beef teriyaki burgers with sizzling vegetables

1/2010
Jerry
doesn't
like.

ingredients

1 lb/450 g best ground steak

8 scallions

2–4 garlic cloves

1-inch/2.5-cm piece fresh gingerroot, grated

½ tsp wasabi or freshly grated horseradish, or to taste

4 tsp teriyaki sauce or marinade

2 tsp peanut oil

4 oz/115 g carrot, grated

4 oz/115 g bok choy, shredded

2 oz/55 g cucumber, shredded

one Place the ground steak, scallions, garlic, ginger, wasabi, and 3 teaspoons of the teriyaki sauce in a food processor and, using the pulse button, blend together. Shape into 4 equal-size burgers, then cover and let chill for 30 minutes.

two Heat a heavy-bottom skillet and add 1 teaspoon of the oil. When hot, add the burgers and cook over medium heat for 3–5 minutes on each side, or according to personal preference. Keep warm.

three Heat a wok and when really hot add the remaining oil. Add the carrots and stir-fry for 1 minute, then add the bok choy, cucumber, and the remaining teriyaki sauce and stir-fry for an additional 1–2 minutes, or until cooked but still crunchy. Serve.

recommended servings

Place the stir-fried vegetables on top of 4 lightly toasted sesame seed baps, top with the cooked burgers, and add some crispy sautéed seaweed. Serve with either a glass of iced tea, freshly brewed green tea, or a glass of Fresh Lemonade (see page 89).

prepare 10 minutes, plus 30 minutes' chilling
cook 15–20 minutes   *serves* 4

For an extra spicy kick to this delicious variation on the classic cheeseburger, place a good spoonful of English mustard on top of the cooked burger before adding the slice of cheese.

the ultimate cheeseburger

ingredients

1 lb/450 g best ground steak
4 onions
2–4 garlic cloves, crushed
2–3 tsp grated fresh horseradish or
 1–1½ tbsp creamed horseradish

pepper
8 lean Canadian bacon slices
2 tbsp corn oil
4 cheese slices (see recommended
 servings)

one Place the ground steak in a large bowl. Finely grate 1 of the onions and add to the ground steak in the bowl.

two Add the garlic, horseradish, and pepper to the steak mixture in the bowl. Mix together, then shape into 4 equal-size burgers. Wrap each burger in 2 slices of bacon, then cover and let chill for 30 minutes.

three Preheat the broiler to medium-high. Slice the remaining onions. Heat the oil in a skillet. Add the onions and cook over medium heat for 8–10 minutes, stirring frequently, until the onions are golden brown. Drain on paper towels and keep warm.

four Cook the burgers under the hot broiler for 3–5 minutes on each side or until cooked to personal preference. Serve.

recommended servings
Toast 4 sesame seed buns. Arrange shredded romaine lettuce on their bases. Add the burgers, sautéed onion, a spoonful of relish, and a cheese slice. Flash broil for 1–2 minutes. Add the lid and serve with extra relish, french fries, and a glass of Fresh Lemonade (see page 89).

Handle fresh chilies with care. Using a small sharp knife, slit the chili down its length and scrape out the seeds and membrane. Place the chili on a board and chop. Wash your hands thoroughly.

chili burgers with cilantro and scallions

ingredients

7 oz/200 g canned red kidney beans, drained and rinsed
1 lb/450 g best ground steak
1–2 fresh red chilies, such as jalapeño, seeded and chopped, or to taste
2–4 garlic cloves, crushed
6 scallions, chopped
1 tbsp chopped fresh cilantro
salt and pepper

salsa
3 ripe tomatoes, peeled and finely chopped
1 small ripe avocado, peeled, pitted, and mashed
4 scallions, finely chopped
1 fresh red jalapeño chili, seeded and finely chopped
1 tbsp chopped fresh cilantro

one Place the kidney beans in a food processor and blend for 1 minute.

two Add the ground steak, chilies, garlic, scallions, cilantro, and salt and pepper to the food processor and blend for an additional 2 minutes. Shape into 4 equal-size burgers, then cover and let chill for 30 minutes.

three Meanwhile, make the salsa. Mix the tomatoes, avocado, scallions, chili, and cilantro together. Place in a small bowl, cover, and let stand for at least 30 minutes to allow the flavors to develop.

four Heat a nonstick skillet until hot. When hot, add the burgers and cook over medium heat for 3–5 minutes on each side, until golden or until cooked to personal preference. Serve with the salsa.

recommended servings
Heat 4 corn tortilla shells according to the package instructions, fill with shredded lettuce and grated carrot and then the burgers. Top with the salsa and sour cream. Serve with tortilla chips and a Melon Smoothie (see page 91).

What could be better for fans of the blt than a blt burger? The asparagus and avocado dip adds that extra taste dimension. When making dips or salsas, prepare them at least 30 minutes before using.

blt burgers

ingredients

8 oz/225 g Canadian bacon slices
1 lb/450 g best ground steak
1 onion, grated
2–4 garlic cloves, crushed
salt and pepper
1–2 tbsp corn oil

dip
6 oz/175 g baby asparagus spears
1 small ripe avocado, peeled, pitted, and finely chopped
1 tbsp lemon juice
2 firm tomatoes, peeled, seeded, and finely chopped
⅔ cup sour cream
salt and pepper

one Remove any rind and fat from the bacon slices and chop finely.

two Place the bacon, ground steak, onion, and garlic in a large bowl and mix well. Shape into 4–6 equal-size burgers, then cover and let chill for 30 minutes.

three Trim the asparagus and cook in a pan of lightly salted boiling water for 5 minutes, then drain and plunge into cold water. When cold, drain and finely chop half the spears into a bowl. Sprinkle the lemon juice over the avocado. Stir in the avocado, tomatoes, and sour cream. Add salt and pepper to taste, cover, and let chill until required.

four Heat a heavy-bottom skillet and add the oil. When hot, add the burgers and cook over medium heat for 5–6 minutes on each side or until cooked to personal preference. Serve.

recommended servings
Arrange lettuce greens over the bases of 4–6 toasted buns, add the burgers, the reserved asparagus, and some tomato slices. Place a spoonful of Dip on top, add the lid, and serve with french fries, the remaining dip and a glass of Tropical Crush (see page 93).

Savory cheese and sweet apple always seem to bring out the best in each other. Here they work their magic in a burger, adding melting texture and sharp flavor to the tender beef.

cheese and apple burgers

ingredients

1 lb/450 g best ground steak	2 oz/55 g sharp Cheddar cheese, grated
1 onion, finely chopped	2 Bramley apples
1–2 tsp whole-grain mustard, or to taste	1 tsp butter, melted
pepper	2–3 tsp superfine sugar
2–3 tsp Worcestershire sauce	2 oz/55 g Gruyère cheese, thinly sliced

one Place the ground steak in a large bowl. Add the onion, mustard, pepper, Worcestershire sauce to taste, and the grated cheese. Peel and core 1 of the apples, then grate and add to the bowl. Mix together, then shape into 4 equal-size burgers. Cover and let chill for 30 minutes.

two Preheat the broiler to medium-high. Peel and core the remaining apple whole, then cut into 4–6 thick slices. Brush with melted butter and sprinkle with the superfine sugar. Place on a foil-lined broiler rack and cook under the hot broiler for 2–3 minutes on each side or until caramelized. Set aside.

three Cook the burgers under the hot broiler for 4–6 minutes on each side or until cooked to personal preference. Top the burgers with the sliced cheese and broil until the cheese has melted. Serve.

recommended servings
Lightly toast 4–6 whole-wheat buns, top with some baby spinach leaves, and the burgers. Place the apple slices on top. Spoon over a little pickle and serve with a mixed salad and a Fruit Milk Shake (see page 87).

prepare 20 minutes, plus 30 minutes' chilling
cook 10–15 minutes *serves* 4

Ring the changes and use mozzarella cheese, fontina, Bel Paese, or even Gorgonzola in this recipe. These delicious burgers are ideal served as part of a barbecue party or an informal supper dish.

italian steak melt burgers

ingredients

1 lb/450 g best ground steak
1 onion, grated
2–4 garlic cloves, crushed
1 small red bell pepper, seeded, peeled, and chopped
⅓ cup pitted black olives, finely chopped

pepper
1 tbsp tomato paste
2 large tomatoes, thickly sliced
3 oz/85 g Gruyère cheese, sliced

one Place the ground steak, onion, garlic, red bell pepper, olives, pepper and tomato paste in a food processor and, using the pulse button, blend together. Shape into 4 equal-size burgers, then cover and let chill for at least 30 minutes.

two Preheat the broiler to medium-high. Place the burgers on a foil-lined broiler rack and cook under the hot broiler for 3–5 minutes on each side or until cooked to personal preference.

three Place a tomato slice on top of each burger, then place the cheese over the tomato. Broil for an additional 2–3 minutes, or until the cheese starts to melt. Serve.

recommended servings
Place some radicchio and arugula leaves on the bases of 4 lightly toasted ciabatta rolls. Drizzle with a little balsamic vinegar. Place the burgers on top, sprinkle some Parmesan cheese shavings over them, place the lid in position, and serve with Ginger Beer (see page 95).

When vegetarian recipes are mentioned, meat-eaters often groan and think just of beans and nuts. Well, the following recipes should silence such sceptics. They make the most of the many diverse ingredients now so readily available in supermarkets. Choose from burgers featuring sweet potatoes, yams, bulgur wheat, or assorted rice with a plethora of herbs, spices, and vegetables. Whichever your choice it is sure to be an all-round winner.

vegetarian

prepare 10–12 minutes, plus 1 hour chilling
cook 30–35 minutes *serves* 4–6

This is a fantastic vegetarian burger, full of flavor, texture, and healthy foods. You can, if you like, substitute the flageolets (green kidney beans) for black-eye peas or red kidney beans.

the ultimate vegetarian burger

ingredients

scant ½ cup brown rice
salt and pepper
14 oz/400 g canned flageolets, drained
scant 1 cup unsalted cashews
3 garlic cloves
1 red onion, cut into wedges

½ cup corn kernels
2 tbsp tomato paste
1 tbsp chopped fresh oregano
2 tbsp whole-wheat flour
2 tbsp corn oil

one Cook the rice in a pan of lightly salted boiling water for 20 minutes, or until tender. Drain and place in a food processor.

two Add the beans, cashews, garlic, onion, corn, tomato paste, oregano, and salt and pepper to the rice in the food processor and, using the pulse button, blend together. Shape into 4–6 equal-size burgers, then coat in the flour. Cover and let chill for 1 hour.

three Heat a heavy-bottom skillet and add the oil. When hot, add the burgers and cook over medium heat for 5–6 minutes on each side or until cooked and piping hot. Serve.

recommended servings
Shred a few romaine lettuce leaves and arrange on the bases of 4–6 lightly toasted whole-wheat buns. Add the burgers, 1–2 tomato slices, and a slice of provolone cheese. Flash broil for 2 minutes, or until the cheese starts to melt. Add the lid and serve with chutney.

prepare 10 minutes, plus 1 hour chilling
cook 10–12 minutes *serves* 4–6

If you are feeling adventurous, try using a hotter variety of fresh chili in the burgers, such as a small Scotch Bonnet, habañero, or even Thai chili. Remember to seed them before using.

three-bean burgers with green mayo

ingredients

10½ oz/300 g canned cannellini beans, drained

10½ oz/300 g canned black-eye peas, drained

10½ oz/300 g canned red kidney beans, drained and rinsed

1 fresh red chili, deseeded

4 shallots, cut into quarters

2 celery stalks, coarsely chopped

1 cup fresh whole-wheat bread crumbs

1 tbsp chopped fresh cilantro

salt and pepper

2 tbsp whole-wheat flour

2 tbsp corn oil

green mayo

6 tbsp prepared mayonnaise

2 tbsp chopped fresh parsley or mint

1 tbsp chopped cucumber

3 scallions, finely chopped

one Place the beans, chili, shallots, celery, bread crumbs, cilantro, and salt and pepper in a food processor and, using the pulse button, blend together. Shape into 4–6 equal-size burgers, then cover and let chill for 1 hour. Coat the burgers lightly in the flour.

two Heat a heavy-bottom skillet and add the oil. When hot, add the burgers and cook over medium heat for 5–6 minutes on each side or until cooked and piping hot.

three Place the mayonnaise, parsley, cucumber, and scallions in a bowl and mix together. Serve.

recommended servings
Serve on a few spinach leaves on the bases of 4–6 lightly toasted sesame seed buns with wedges of charred red and yellow bell peppers. Spoon over a little Green Mayo and a little salsa. Place the lid on top. Serve with potato wedges and a glass of Ginger Beer (see page 95).

prepare 10 minutes, plus 1 hour chilling
cook 25–35 minutes *serves* 4–6

In this recipe the burgers have a smooth texture, but if you prefer them to be chunkier, blend the mixture only briefly and do not peel the bell peppers.

yam and red bell pepper burgers

ingredients

8 oz/225 g yam, peeled and cut into chunks
salt and pepper
14 oz/400 g canned chickpeas, drained
2 red bell peppers, seeded and peeled
2–3 garlic cloves, crushed

½ cup pitted black olives
2 tbsp sesame seeds
1 tbsp chopped fresh cilantro
2 tbsp whole-wheat flour
2 tbsp corn oil

one Cook the yam in a pan of lightly salted boiling water for 15–20 minutes, or until tender. Drain well and place in a food processor.

two Add the chickpeas, red bell peppers, garlic, olives, sesame seeds, cilantro, and salt and pepper to the yam in the food processor and, using the pulse button, blend together. Shape into 4–6 equal-size burgers, then coat in the flour. Cover and let chill for 1 hour.

three Heat a heavy-bottom skillet and add the oil. When hot, add the burgers and cook over medium heat for 5–6 minutes on each side or until cooked and piping hot. Serve.

recommended servings
Arrange some arugula leaves on the bases of 4–6 lightly toasted cheese-topped buns and add the burgers. Spoon over some hummus and a little tomato salsa. Add the lid and serve with a green salad, tortilla chips, and a Mango Smoothie (see page 91).

A large root vegetable similar to celery, celeriac is ideal for these burgers since it gives an excellent flavor as well as adding texture. Firm up the burgers in the refrigerator before coating in the flour.

butternut squash with cornmeal burgers

ingredients

1 lb/450 g butternut squash (8 oz/225 g after peeling and seeding), cut into chunks

⅔ cup water

generous ½ cup instant cornmeal

4 oz/115 g celeriac, peeled and grated

6 scallions, finely chopped

1 cup pecans, chopped

½ cup freshly grated Parmesan cheese

2 tbsp chopped fresh mixed herbs

salt and pepper

2 tbsp whole-wheat flour

2 tbsp corn oil

one Cook the butternut squash in a pan of boiling water for 15–20 minutes, or until tender. Drain and finely chop or mash. Place the water in a separate pan and bring to a boil. Slowly pour in the cornmeal in a steady stream and cook over gentle heat, stirring, for 5 minutes, or until thick.

two Remove the pan from the heat and stir in the butternut squash, celeriac, scallions, pecans, cheese, herbs, and salt and pepper to taste. Mix well, then shape into 4–6 equal-size burgers. Cover and let chill for at least 1 hour. Coat the burgers lightly in the flour.

three Heat a heavy-bottom skillet and add the oil. When hot, add the burgers and cook over medium heat for 5–6 minutes on each side or until cooked and piping hot. Serve.

recommended servings

Place a few watercress sprigs on the bases of 4–6 cheese-topped baps, top with the burgers, and sliced tomato. Squeeze over some tomato ketchup, add the lid, and serve with extra tomato ketchup, french fries, coleslaw, and a Fruit Milk Shake (see page 87).

prepare 10–12 minutes, plus 1 hour chilling
cook 40–45 minutes *serves* 4–6

There are lots of interesting textures and flavors vying for your attention in these tasty burgers. For an extra cheesy kick, pan-fry some slices of provolone cheese to serve on top of the burgers.

sweet potato and provolone burgers

ingredients

1 lb/450 g sweet potatoes, peeled and
  cut into chunks
salt and pepper
6 oz/175 g broccoli florets
2–3 garlic cloves, crushed
1 red onion, finely chopped or grated
1½–2 fresh red jalapeño chilies, seeded
  and finely chopped

6 oz/175 g provolone cheese, grated
2 tbsp whole-wheat flour
2–3 tbsp corn oil
1 lb/450 g onions, sliced
1 tbsp chopped fresh cilantro

one Cook the sweet potato in a pan of lightly salted boiling water for 15–20 minutes, or until tender. Drain and mash. Cut the broccoli into small pieces, cook in a separate pan of boiling water for 3 minutes, then drain and plunge into cold water. Drain again, then add to the mashed sweet potato.

two Stir in the garlic, red onion, chili, grated cheese, and salt and pepper. Mix well and shape into 4–6 equal-size burgers, then coat in the flour. Cover and let chill for at least 1 hour.

three Heat 1½ tablespoons of the oil in a heavy-bottom skillet. Add the onions with any remaining chili and cook over medium heat for 12–15 minutes, or until softened. Stir in the cilantro and set aside.

four Add the remaining oil to the skillet. Add the burgers and cook over medium heat for 5–6 minutes on each side or until piping hot. Serve with the onions.

recommended servings

Place some bitter salad greens on the bases of 4–6 lightly toasted whole-wheat buns, top with the burgers, the onions, some sweet chili or hot pepper sauce. Add the lid and serve with ice tea or Fresh Lemonade (see page 89).

Tofu is made from soybeans and since it has very little flavor it will easily absorb any flavor it is combined with. It is an excellent source of protein and is ideal for vegetarians.

vegetable and tofu burgers

ingredients

generous ½ cup Thai rice
4 oz/115 g carrot, grated
6 scallions, coarsely chopped
scant ½ cup unsalted peanuts
generous ½ cup fresh bean sprouts

8 oz/225 g firm tofu (drained weight), finely chopped
1 tsp prepared ginger pulp
½–1 tsp crushed chilies
1–2 tbsp corn oil

one Cook the rice in a pan of lightly boiling water for 12–15 minutes, or until soft. Drain and place in a large bowl.

two Place the carrot, scallions and peanuts in a food processor and, using the pulse button, chop finely. Add the rice, bean sprouts, tofu, ginger, and chilies and blend together. Shape into 4–6 equal-size burgers, firmly pressing them together. Cover and let chill for 1 hour.

three Heat a heavy-bottom skillet and add the oil. When hot, add the burgers and cook over medium heat for 5–6 minutes on each side or until piping hot. Serve.

recommended servings

Place shredded bok choy and fresh bean sprouts on the bases of 4–6 lightly toasted sesame seed buns and top with the burgers. Add lightly sautéed oyster and shiitake mushrooms and drizzle over some satay sauce. Add the lid. Serve with an Asian-style salad.

prepare 15 minutes, plus 1 hour chilling
cook 30–35 minutes *serves* 4–6

If eating alfresco, serve these burgers as part of a light lunch out in the garden or for supper. In winter try them for brunch with plenty of salad and warm crusty bread.

mushroom, spinach, and rice burgers

ingredients

2 tbsp mixed basmati and wild rice

2–3 tbsp olive oil

3–4 garlic cloves, crushed

10½ oz/300 g white mushrooms, chopped

3¾ cups fresh spinach leaves

10½ oz/300 g canned cranberry beans, drained

1 orange bell pepper, seeded, peeled, and finely chopped

½ cup slivered almonds, toasted

2 oz/55 g Parmesan cheese, freshly grated

2 tbsp chopped fresh basil

1 cup fresh whole-wheat bread crumbs

salt and pepper

2 tbsp whole-wheat flour

1–2 beefsteak tomatoes, thickly sliced

one Cook the rice in a pan of boiling water for 12–15 minutes, or until tender. Drain and place in a large bowl.

two Heat 1 tablespoon of the oil in a skillet. Add the garlic and mushrooms and cook for 5 minutes. Add to the rice in the bowl.

three Reserve ⅝ cup spinach leaves. Take the remaining spinach and lightly rinse and pat the leaves completely dry. Place the spinach, beans, bell pepper, almonds, Parmesan cheese, basil, bread crumbs, and salt and pepper in a food processor and, using the pulse button, chop finely. Mix well, then shape into 4–6 equal-size burgers. Coat in the flour, then cover and let chill for 1 hour.

four Heat a heavy-bottom skillet and add the remaining oil. When hot, add the burgers and cook over medium heat for 5–6 minutes on each side or until piping hot. Add the tomato slices for the last 3 minutes of cooking to heat through, then serve.

recommended servings
Place each burger on a lightly sautéed large portobello mushroom, sitting on a bed of spinach, topped with the cooked tomato slices. Serve with a glass of Ginger Beer (see page 95).

prepare 20 minutes, plus 1 hour chilling
cook 25–30 minutes *serves* 4–6

There is a great variety of textures and flavors wrapped up in these chili burgers. To maximize the cilantro's contribution, chop the root and stalks into the mixture as well as the leaves.

vegetarian chili burgers

ingredients

½ cup bulgur wheat

salt and pepper

10½ oz/300 g canned red kidney beans, drained and rinsed

10½ oz/300 g canned cannellini beans, drained

1–2 fresh red jalapeño chilies, seeded and coarsely chopped

2–3 garlic cloves

6 scallions, coarsely chopped

1 yellow bell pepper, seeded, peeled, and chopped

1 tbsp chopped fresh cilantro

4 oz/115 g mature Cheddar cheese, grated

2 tbsp whole-wheat flour

1–2 tbsp corn oil

1 large tomato, sliced

one Cook the bulgur wheat in a pan of lightly salted water for 12 minutes, or until cooked. Drain and set aside.

two Place the beans in a food processor with the chilies, garlic, scallions, pepper, cilantro, and half the cheese. Using the pulse button, chop finely. Add to the cooked bulgur wheat with salt and pepper to taste. Mix well, then shape into 4–6 equal-size burgers. Cover and let chill for 1 hour. Coat the burgers in the flour.

three Preheat the broiler to medium. Heat a heavy-bottom skillet and add the oil. When hot, add the burgers and cook over medium heat for 5–6 minutes on each side or until piping hot.

four Place 1–2 slices of tomato on top of each burger and sprinkle with the remaining cheese. Cook under the hot broiler for 2–3 minutes, or until the cheese starts to melt. Serve.

recommended servings

Serve on salad greens with 1–2 tablespoons of warmed refried beans on 4–6 whole-wheat baps. Add a sprinkle of cheese on top. Spoon over some sour cream and add the lid. Serve with pickled chilies, an avocado and tomato salad, and Fresh Lemonade (see page 89).

Blue cheese can be a domineering flavor, but not when mixed with apples and nuts in a burger like this. Since they are all refrigerator and pantry ingredients you can make this recipe at any time.

blue cheese and apple burgers

ingredients

6 oz/175 g new potatoes

scant 1½ cups mixed nuts, such as
   pecans, almonds, and hazelnuts

1 onion, coarsely chopped

8 oz/225 g Granny Smith or other eating
   apples, peeled, cored, and grated

6 oz/175 g blue cheese, such as Stilton,
   crumbled

1 cup fresh whole-wheat bread crumbs

salt and pepper

2 tbsp whole-wheat flour

1–2 tbsp corn oil

one Cook the potatoes in a pan of boiling water for 15–20 minutes, or until tender when pierced with a fork. Drain and, using a potato masher, crush into small pieces. Place in a large bowl.

two Place the nuts and onion in a food processor and, using the pulse button, chop finely. Add the nuts, onion, apple, cheese, and bread crumbs to the potatoes in the bowl. Season with salt and pepper to taste. Mix well, then shape into 4–6 equal-size burgers. Coat in the flour, then cover and let chill for 1 hour.

three Heat a heavy-bottom skillet and add the oil. When hot, add the burgers and cook over medium heat for 5–6 minutes on each side or until piping hot. Serve.

recommended servings

Arrange salad greens on top of the bases of 4–6 lightly toasted cheese-topped buns. Add the burger. Top with sliced red onions, add the lid, and serve with coleslaw, tomato ketchup, and a Chocolate Milk Shake (see page 87).

When silky smooth macadamias meet feisty feta cheese, probably for the first time ever in this burger mixture, it turns out to be a winning combination.

macadamia and feta cheese burgers

ingredients

generous ½ cup Thai rice

salt and pepper

1½ cups macadamias

1 red onion, cut into wedges

1 red bell pepper, seeded and chopped

1 tbsp fresh chopped cilantro

8 oz/225 g feta cheese

2 tbsp whole-wheat flour

1 egg, beaten

1½ cups fresh whole-wheat bread crumbs

1–2 tbsp corn oil

one Cook the rice in a pan of lightly salted boiling water for 12 minutes, or until tender. Drain well and set aside.

two Place the nuts, red onion, bell pepper, and cilantro in a food processor and, using the pulse button, chop finely, then add to the rice. Crumble the cheese finely, then add to the mixture with salt and pepper to taste. Shape into 4–6 equal-size burgers, then coat in the flour, cover, and let chill for 1 hour.

three Place the egg and bread crumbs in 2 separate bowls and coat the burgers first in the egg, allowing any excess to drip back into the bowl, then in the bread crumbs.

four Heat a heavy-bottom skillet and add the oil. When hot, add the burgers and cook over medium heat for 5–6 minutes on each side or until piping hot. Serve.

recommended servings

Serve the burgers with strips of warm pita bread, sweet chili sauce, and a couscous salad mixed with chopped bell peppers, raisins, and chopped fresh cilantro and a Chocolate Milk Shake (see page 87).

It makes a refreshing change to create your own drinks to accompany a meal, and when you do so you can be assured that the ingredients are the very best, whether you are making a zingy fresh lemonade or a fruity, honey-sweetened smoothie. The drinks in this chapter go extremely well with burgers, and most are, like the burgers, quick and straightforward to make. The notable exception is Ginger Beer, which takes a couple of weeks.

drinks

For chocolate lovers, a good chocolate milk shake is heaven in a glass. To make an even richer shake, in place of the drinking chocolate, whisk melted semisweet chocolate into the ice-cold milk.

chocolate milk shake

ingredients

1 heaping tbsp drinking chocolate
1 tsp superfine sugar, or to taste
  (optional)
2 tsp just-boiled water
1¼ cups ice-cold milk
1 scoop each of good-quality vanilla
  and chocolate ice cream

one Reserve ½ teaspoon of drinking chocolate, then place the remainder in a small bowl with the superfine sugar, if using. Blend to a smooth paste with the water.

two Place in a blender with the milk and 1 of the scoops of ice cream. Blend for 1 minute, then pour into a tall glass, add the remaining ice cream, sprinkle the reserved drinking chocolate over the mixture, and serve.

FRUIT-FLAVORED MILK SHAKES

Fruit-flavored milk shakes can be easily made as follows: Purée scant ½ cup of fresh or thawed raspberries and place in a blender with the milk. Float a scoop or two of ice cream, such as vanilla or strawberry, on top, or pipe a swirl of whipped cream over the top with extra fruits. Use 1–2 mashed ripe bananas and top with a scoop of frozen yogurt and a sprinkle of ground cinnamon or a few flakes of fresh coconut.

variation
You can add grated nutmeg or a little ground cinnamon to the blender and sprinkle sparingly on top of the ice cream.

prepare 15 minutes, plus 3 hours' standing
cook 0 minutes *makes* 1.2 litres/2 pints

There is nothing more refreshing on a hot summer's day than a glass or two of homemade lemonade—there is, of course, the added bonus that there are no artificial additives.

fresh lemonade

ingredients

4 large lemons, preferably
  unwaxed or organic
scant 1 cup superfine sugar
3½ cups boiling water
ice cubes, to serve

one Scrub the lemons well and dry. Using a vegetable peeler, peel 3 of the lemons very thinly. Place the peel in a large pitcher or bowl, add the sugar and boiling water, and stir well until the sugar has dissolved. Cover the pitcher and let stand for at least 3 hours, stirring occasionally. Meanwhile, squeeze the juice from the lemons and set aside.

two Strain the lemon peel and stir in the reserved lemon juice. Thinly slice the remaining lemon and cut the slices in half. Add to the lemonade together with the ice cubes. Stir and serve.

variation
You can try using oranges or limes or a mixture of all 3 fruits for some equally refreshing thirst-quenchers.

Make sure that the mango is ripe. Canned mango would work but drain thoroughly and omit the honey. For a change use half orange and half lime juice and sprinkle with a little ground cinnamon.

mango smoothie

ingredients

1 mango, peeled, seeded, and sliced

1 tsp honey, or to taste (optional)

scant 1 cup freshly squeezed orange
 juice

2 tbsp plain yogurt

5–6 ice cubes

one Place the mango in a blender with the honey and orange juice. Blend for 1 minute, then add the yogurt with the ice cubes and blend for an additional 1 minute.

two Pour into a tall glass and serve with a straw.

variation

Melon Smoothie can be made by using 3 different seeded and peeled melons. Try watermelon, galia, and charentais with plenty of crushed ice and a few slices of strawberry on top.

Tropical fruits have particularly exotic flavors but you can use any mixture of fruits to make a crush: a medley of summer berries or citrus fruits is very colorful and thirst-quenching too.

tropical crush

ingredients

1 ripe papaya, peeled, seeded, and
  chopped
1 banana, peeled and sliced
⅔ cup mango and orange juice
4 tbsp passion fruit and peach yogurt
5–6 ice cubes
lime slices, to decorate

one Place both fruits in a blender with the mango and orange juice, yogurt, and ice cubes. Blend for 1 minute, or until well blended and frothy.

two Pour into a tall glass and decorate with slices of lime. Serve.

variation
Try adding a measure of rum for an adult version.

Although this drink takes a while to get started the first time, it is well worth the wait. By the time you have drunk the first batch, your second is well on the way.

ginger beer

ingredients

plant

1 oz/25 g fresh yeast or ½ oz/15 g
   dried yeast

1¼ cups water

9 tsp white sugar

9 tsp ground ginger

beer

2 lb/900 g granulated sugar

2½ cups hot water

16 cups cold water

juice of 2 large lemons, strained

one Place the yeast in a clean dry jar or similar container. Pour over the water and stir in 2 teaspoons of the white sugar and 2 teaspoons of the ground ginger. Cover lightly with plastic wrap and leave in a cool dark place.

two Next day, stir in an additional 1 teaspoon of sugar and 1 teaspoon of ground ginger. Repeat this for the next 7 days.

three Strain the plant through cheesecloth and use half the sediment to begin a new plant in a large jar.

four To make the beer, dissolve the granulated sugar in the hot water, stirring until completely dissolved. Top up with the cold water, the strained lemon juice, and the strained plant. Stir well and pour into clean screw-top bottles. Screw down tightly and let stand in a cool dark place for 1 week before drinking.

variation

Make a refreshing summer drink by pouring
⅔ cup of the ginger beer into a tall glass
a quarter full of crushed ice, top off with lemonade,
and float a scoop of vanilla ice cream on top.

index

apples
blue cheese and apple
burgers 81
cheese and apple burgers 59

bacon
bacon-wrapped chicken
burgers 27
blt burgers 57
chicken and bacon burgers 35
barbecued cajun pork
burgers 39
beans
three-bean burgers with
green mayo 67
beef
beef teriyaki burgers with
sizzling vegetables 51
chili burgers with cilantro
and scallions 55
classic hamburger, the 49
italian steak melt burgers 61
blt burgers 57
blue cheese and apple
burgers 81
butternut squash with cornmeal
burgers 71

cheese
blue cheese and apple
burgers 81
cheese and apple burgers 59
lamb and feta cheese
burgers 43
macadamia and feta cheese
burgers 83
sweet potato and provolone
burgers 73
ultimate cheeseburger,
the 53
chicken
bacon-wrapped chicken
burgers 27
chicken and bacon burgers 35
ultimate chicken burger,
the 23
chili burgers with cilantro
and scallions 55
chocolate milk shake 87
classic hamburger, the 49

cod
provençal cod burgers 11
cornmeal
butternut squash with
cornmeal burgers 71
crab
thai crab burgers with bean
sprouts 13

drink recipes 84–95
duck burgers with sweet apple
and plum relish 31

fish burgers 19
fish recipes 6–19
fresh lemonade 89
fresh tuna burgers with mango
salsa 17

ginger beer 95

italian steak melt burgers 61

lamb
lamb and feta cheese
burgers 43
lamb tikka masala burgers 47
minty lamb burgers 45

macadamia and feta cheese
burgers 83
mango
fresh tuna burgers with
mango salsa 17
mango smoothie 91
maple-glazed turkey burgers 33
meat recipes 36–61
mexican turkey burgers 25
minty lamb burgers 45
mushroom, spinach, and
rice burgers 77

pork
barbecued cajun pork
burgers 39
pork burgers with tangy
orange marinade 41
poultry recipes 20–35
provençal cod burgers 11

red bell peppers
yam and red bell pepper
burgers 69

salmon
crispy salmon burgers with
pine nuts 15
smoky trout burgers with
pesto relish 9
sweet potato and provolone
burgers 73

thai crab burgers with
bean sprouts 13
three-bean burgers with
green mayo 67
tofu
vegetable and tofu
burgers 75
tropical crush 93
trout
smoky trout burgers with
pesto relish 9
tuna
fresh tuna burgers with
mango salsa 17
turkey
maple-glazed turkey
burgers 33
mexican turkey burgers 25
turkey and tarragon burgers
29

ultimate cheeseburger, the 53
ultimate chicken burger, the 23
ultimate vegetarian burger,
the 65

vegetables
beef teriyaki burgers with
sizzling vegetables 51
vegetable and tofu burgers 75
vegetarian chili burgers 79
vegetarian recipes 62–83

yam and red bell pepper
burgers 69